Historic Street Scenes
of Kansas City, Missouri
1867 - 1931

featuring the *Val B. Mintun Photography Collection*

by **Raymond S. Elder,** *Historian*
KC Fire Historical Society

M.T. Publishing Company, Inc.
P.O. Box 6802
Evansville, Indiana 47719-6802
www.mtpublishing.com

Copyright © 2011
Raymond S. Elder

Graphic Designer: Amanda Reyher

All rights reserved. No part of this publication may be translated, reproduced, or transmitted in any form or by any means, electronic or mechanical, including photocopying and recording, or by any information storage and retrieval system, without expressed written permission of the copyright owner and M.T. Publishing Company, Inc.

The materials were compiled and produced using available information; M.T. Publishing Company, Inc., and the copyright holder regret they cannot assume liability for errors or omissions.

Library of Congress Control Number: 2011927632

ISBN: 978-1-934729-64-9

Printed in the United States of America

Cover Photo: Willis Wood Theatre

Contents

About This Book	3
Acknowledgements	3
Raymond S. Elder	3
Val B. Mintun	4
1870's	6
1880's	10
1890's	27
1900's	46
1910's	47
1920's	63
1930's	70
Postcards	71

About This Book

You are about to view a collection of some photographs that have not been seen in over one-hundred years and to read the story of how this book came into being.

In mid April of 2010 a long time friend and co-worker Joseph D. Galetti, a retired Fire Captain of the Kansas City Fire Department, asked if I would advise him on what could be done with about 100 old photographs that belonged to his great grandfather Val B. Mintun.

In reviewing the photographs I was positive this was a small treasure of historical photographs of Kansas City, Missouri. I suggested to Mr. Galetti the possibility of the photographs being published in book form, he readily agreed and I began compiling this book.

Mr. Mintun's collection came about by the photographs he took, photographs he purchased or were given to him. On the back of most of the photographs he penciled in a general description, where it was taken and sometimes a date. The identification of photographs without his notes was identified by a business name or other objects in the photo. Some were identified by other photographs. (i.e. The Corn-Belt Bank on page 47 identified the street intersection on page 57.)

The photographs in this collection that were not used were faded beyond use. My only regret is not being able to save the faded or identify all the photographs. There are some great photographs of Kansas City, Missouri history. Through the medium of photography is how I was introduced to Mr. Galetti's great grandfather Mr. Val B. Mintun. Enjoy the Mintun Collection.

Raymond S. Elder, *Historian*
KC Fire Historical Society
2011 January

Acknowledgements

In compiling this book there are four people I have relied on immensely. My wife, Nancy L. Elder, Mark Trued, John Broski and Michael G. Bushnell, Editor and Publisher of the Northeast News of Kansas City Missouri. It would require several pages to tell of your assistance and guidance. Thanks for your help.

Raymond S. Elder

Ray served 35 years with the Kansas City Fire Department rising to the rank of Captain in 1977 and retiring July 28, 1993.

His life long hobby of collecting and studying the history of the Kansas City Fire Department has produced 4 books.

He is a native of Kansas City, Missouri and is a member of and/or officer in the following organizations: Historian for the KC Fire Historical Society; Vice President of the Kansas City Retired Fire Fighters Association; Active retiree of Local 42 of the IAFF; Member of the Native Sons and Daughters of Kansas City; Jackson County Historical Society: Union Cemetery Historical Society and The Westerners.

Val B. Mintun

Mr. Mintun was born in Kansas City near 14th and Baltimore Streets on August 29, 1874. He was the son of Henry M. Mintun, a pioneer of Jackson County. His father came from Ohio and his mother came from Middletown, Delaware. Mr. Mintun received his education from the public schools of Kansas City, Missouri.

Mr. Mintun's business career revolved around the telephone and one of the earliest known companies he worked for was the Missouri-Kansas Telephone Co. In 1905 he was hired as a salesman and ended his career with the Southwestern Bell Telephone Co. as the District Manager, retiring September 1, 1939.

He had a lifetime hobby of photography, not only taking photographs but purchasing photographs from other photographers. He also became interested in 16mm movie film and some of his work goes back to 1924. He worked with Fire Chiefs John T. Lynch and Harvey L. Baldwin of the Kansas City Fire Department in making a training film for new recruits. (1949-1950)

Mr. Mintun was very strong in civic pride and was a member or officer in many civic organizations. The known organizations were: Masonic Lodge, Thirty-second Degree Mason and Shriner; Member of the Board of Directors of the Commercial Club in 1914, (This is the fore-runner of the Chamber of Commerce); and member and President of the Charles S. Gleed Chapter of the Telephone Pioneers of America in 1928. He also was a member of the Railroad Club, Elks Lodge, Kansas City Club, Mid-Day Club and the Rotarians.

Mr. Mintun was 80 yeas old when he passed away January 24, 1955.

Val B. Mintun circa 1910

Val B. Mintun circa 1913

Photograph to the right: (l to r): Charlie Johnson, Sid Barmidge, Jean Potts, Claude Nichols, Joe Rewely, "Curley", Harry Minton, Joe Boppart, Howard Stark, Frank Dolan, Val B. Mintun, John Dolan and Guy Casey.

Back of photo at the top left. Photo taken about 1894.

Top photograph: The general committee in charge of the First Aid contest held in Kansas City on May 23rd. (l to r) First row: W. R. Nicholson, J. W. Bowdy, C. H. Weiser, F. F. Holmgren and L. C. Fisher. Back row: Val Mintun, Milton Baer, Willard Scherff, Stanley Skinner, H. L. Johnson and H. R. Fritz. **Photograph to the left:** Captains of the six platoons of Red Cross nurses who performed in the grand march at Convention Hall. (l to r) Standing: Elizabeth Stalzer, Mrs. Thelma Parnell and Mrs. Helen Froher. Seated: Ruth Eversole, Anna Moran and Mrs. Mae Moske. **Photograph to the right:** Carrie Lee Thomas, marshal of Red Cross nurses, whose ability as an organizer helped to make the grand march a success.

Jackson County Courthouse

Kansas City, Missouri – Circa 1874
In this photo you are looking north-northeast from one of the upper floors on the north side of the Coates House Hotel, 10th and Broadway Streets. The Jackson County Court House is in the top mid-right of this photograph. (Val B. Mintun Collection)

Kansas City, Missouri – Circa 1874
Looking northwest from the southeast corner of 5th and Main Streets. Hammerslough's Clothing House is the building with the flag pole and had a street address of 412 Main Street. (Val B. Mintun Collection)

Kansas City, Missouri – Circa 1874 Looking at the southwest corner of 5th and Delaware Streets and the entrance to the 1st National Bank. (Val B. Mintun Collection)

Kansas City Missouri – Circa 1874
This is the intersection of 4th and Delaware Streets looking southwest. The E. L. Martin & Co. was located at 404 Delaware Street and sold "Kentucky Whiskey". E. L. Martin was also Mayor of Kansas City in 1873/1874. To the right of the horse carriage is a dog asleep in the street. (Val B. Mintun Collection)

Kansas City, Missouri – Circa 1880
This is the second Live Stock Exchange Building. The sign underneath the clock identifies the building as the: "Kansas City Live Stock Exchange 1876" This building was near 16th and Bell Streets, an area of Kansas City, Missouri known as the West Bottoms. (Val B. Mintun Collection)

Kansas City, Missouri – Circa 1881
Looking east on 8th Street from Grand Avenue. The twin spires of St. Patrick's Catholic Church are shown on the right side of 8th street. To the right of the left spire is a fire watchtower used by the Kansas City, Missouri Fire Department. The watchtower was removed in 1906 and a matching spire replaced the fire watchtower. To the left of St. Patrick's Church is the St. Patrick's Catholic School. (Val B. Mintun Collection)

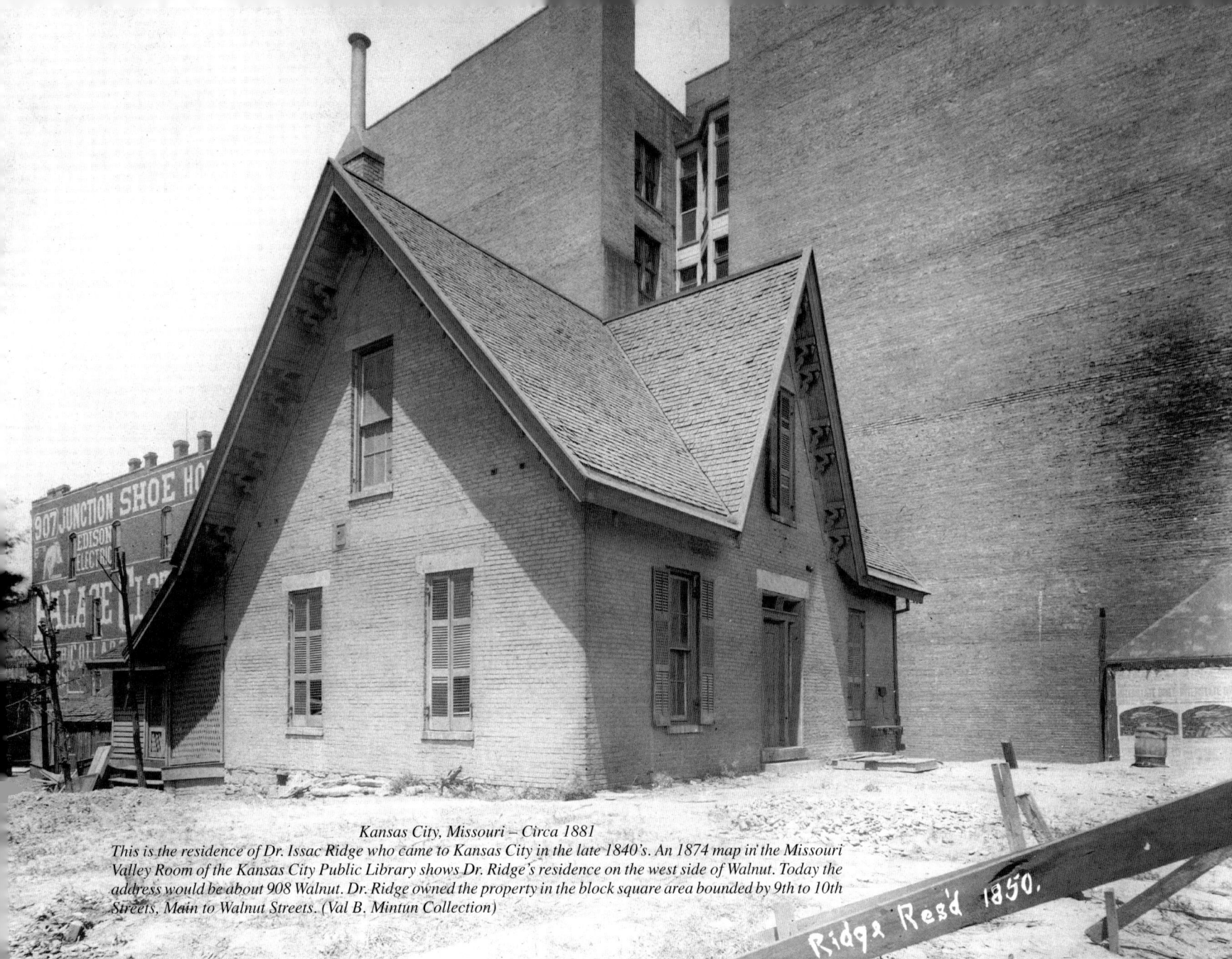

Kansas City, Missouri – Circa 1881
This is the residence of Dr. Issac Ridge who came to Kansas City in the late 1840's. An 1874 map in the Missouri Valley Room of the Kansas City Public Library shows Dr. Ridge's residence on the west side of Walnut. Today the address would be about 908 Walnut. Dr. Ridge owned the property in the block square area bounded by 9th to 10th Streets, Main to Walnut Streets. (Val B. Mintun Collection)

Kansas City, Missouri – 1881
Looking south on Main Street from 5th Street. The fire hydrant located near the bottom of the stairs is a Birdsill Holly fire hydrant. This was the first style of fire hydrant used by the City and they were installed between 1875 and 1881. The houses on top of the hill were torn down and the hill was graded to street level. (Val B. Mintun Collection)

Kansas City, Missouri – Circa 1881

Looking west-northwest and the bend of the Missouri River is on the right hand side of photo. The building marked "Novelty" is grain elevator built in 1879 with a capacity of 225,000 bushels. The 1879 address was listed as the "Missouri Pacific R.R. Tracks and Santa-Fe Street". Today that is the same as 9th and Santa-Fe Streets. The Keystone Iron Works Co. is listed in the City Directory of 1879 with an address of "Union Street near the Union depot." If the building existed today it would have an address of about 1000 W. 8th Street. 8th Street is the unimproved street shown in front of the building. The edge of the Union Elevator is shown on the right side of this photo and can be seen in the next photo. (Val B. Mintun Collection)

Kansas City, Missouri – Circa 1881
Looking north-northwest with the bend of the Missouri River in the background. The Union elevator shown in this photo is the second Union Grain Elevator. The first elevator was destroyed by fire in December of 1873. If this elevator was still standing today an approximate address would be about 800 Woodsweather Road. The Missouri River has signs of floating drift wood which indicates the river is rising. This could be the starting of 1881 flood. (Val B. Mintun Collection)

Kansas City, Missouri – Circa 1881
This photograph is believed to be the flood of 1881. Unable to identify the street other than it one of the major streets in the part of the city known as the "West Bottoms." (Val B. Mintun Collection)

Kansas City, Missouri – "The Junction" Circa 1886
Looking north on Main Street at the Vaughan Diamond Building. This building set in a wedge area between Delaware and Main Streets that intersected at 9th Street. The "Junction" was once considered the center of Kansas City, Missouri. The building was built in 1871 and razed in 1915. (Val B. Mintun Collection)

Kansas City, Missouri – May 11, 1886
A cyclone destroyed the Jackson County Courthouse located at 2nd and Main Streets. The Missouri River is located about two blocks behind the courthouse. Two people were killed and three injured. (Val B. Mintun Collection)

Kansas City, Missouri – Circa 1887
The 8th Street Streetcar Tunnel went into service April 25, 1888 and terminated service April 29, 1956. This tunnel provided a quick way to reach the West Bottoms of Kansas City area. Cable cars were in use up to 1893 then changed to electric trolley cars. The tunnel was temporarily closed from 1922 to 1928 to repair the steel elevated rail line. In this photo you are looking west from the east portal. The west portal exited the bluff on a 20ft. steel elevated rail line. (Val B. Mintun Collection)

Kansas City, Missouri – Circa 1886
An elevated steam engine with two cars that is letting passengers off at one of their depots along their route. This particular train may have been part of the Rosedale Avenue Steam Line. An elevated line did not have to contend with traffic or floods. Most of the elevated lines began near the Union Depot located on Union Avenue near Santa-Fe Street. The engines were made to look like a street car so they would not frighten the horses. Fares were 5 cents and ran on a 15 minute schedule. (Val B. Mintun Collection)

Kansas City, Missouri – Circa 1887– Northeast Corner of 9th & Central
The small house in the center of the photo is on the Northeast corner of 9th and Central Street. The first floor of this house was a small restaurant serving meals for 15 cents. Central Street is in the process of being graded and 9th and Wyandotte Street is on the right of photo. The New England Life building is on the northeast corner and the Beal building is on the northwest corner. The building under construction is the Board of Trade building being erected at 210 West 8th Street. (Val B. Mintun Collection)

Kansas City, Missouri – 1888
Republican Headquarters: Located on the west side of Walnut Street between 11th Street and 12th Street. The gentleman seated on the front row (5th from the left) is Robert T. Van Horn, Mayor of Kansas City, Missouri 1861, 1863 and 1864. (Val B. Mintun Collection)

Kansas City, Missouri – Circa 1888
The 1st Congregational Church located on southeast corner of 11th and McGee Streets. The building of this church was completed in 1884. The church merged with another Congregational church in 1905 and was razed in 1908. Sanborn Fire maps of 1895-1907 shows the church spire to be 148 feet tall. (Val B. Mintun Collection)

Kansas City, Missouri – Circa 1889
The completion of building the Kansas City Pittsburg & Gulf Railway to the "Grand Central Station" train depot located at 2nd and Wyandotte streets. The tracks were laid down the center of 2nd Street from the east. The workmen are replacing Walnut Street going south over the railroad tracks. The depot was opened in 1890. The building in this photo was not identified. The Missouri River can be seen on the left hand side of photo. (Val B. Mintun Collection)

Kansas City, Missouri – Circa Early 1889
Looking at the northeast corner of 11th and Walnut Streets. The beginning of grading and foundation work for the new building of the Bullene-Moore-Emery & Co. (Val B. Mintun Collection)

Kansas City, Missouri – Circa 1889
Looking northeast from the intersection of 11th and Walnut Avenue. The building under construction is the Bullene-Moore-Emery & Co. The future name of this building is the Emery-Bird Thayer Dry Goods Co. The church shown on the right side of the photo is the 1st Congregational Church located on the northeast corner 11th and McGee streets. (Val B. Mintun Collection)

Kansas City, Missouri – Circa 1890
Looking northwest at the southeast corner of 11th and Grand Avenue. Construction began on the new Bullene-Moore-Emery & Co. building in May of 1888 and completed in September of 1890. The company changed names several times over the years and its last name was Emery-Bird-Thayer Department Store. (Val B. Mintun Collection)

Kansas City, Missouri – Circa 1890
This three-story building was located on the northwest corner of 21st Street and Grand Avenue.
The Bruce Lumber Company owned several buildings in the area. (Val B. Mintun Collection)

Kansas City, Missouri – Circa 1890
The Western Sash and Door Company was located on the northwest corner of 23rd and Grand Avenue. The building near the bridge is the Freight Station for the KC Belt Railway. The freight car "Peet Bros. Mfg. Co. Kansas City U.S.A" is one of the companies that merged to become the Colgate-Palmolive-Peet Company, now known as the "Colgate Palmolive Co." (Val B. Mintun Collection)

Kansas City, Missouri – Circa 1890
Beginning construction of City Hall on Main Street between 4th and 5th Streets. The building went into service October 24, 1892 and was demolished in 1938. The building on the left hand side of the photo is the City Market building. The building, center-left, is the Gillis Opera House built in 1883 and destroyed by fire in 1925. 4th Street is at the bottom of the photo with Main Street on the right side. Notice the absence of any construction cranes and how the steel beam is being moved into position with hydraulic jacks. (Val B. Mintun Collection)

Kansas City, Missouri – Circa 1891

This photograph was taken from the roof of the Hotel Victoria, 304 E. 9th Street, looking west. McGee Street is at the bottom of the photograph with 9th street on the left hand side and 8th street on the right hand side. (8th Street is not visible in the photograph) The following buildings are shown in this photograph: Rialto Building at 9th & Grand Avenue; Keith and Perry Building at 9th & Walnut Street; Hotel Midland at 7th and Walnut Street. The houses in the square block area are being razed to build the new U.S. Post Office and Customs House. (Val B. Mintun Collection)

Kansas City, Missouri Circa 1891
Unable to identify the construction site or the street intersection in this photo. Mr. Mintun penciled in the "Board of Trade Building at 8th & Wyandotte" which is not correct. (Val B. Mintun Collection)

Kansas City, Missouri – Circa 1891
Looking west from the roof of a building located at 404 E. 9th Street. The two churches on the left hand side of the Hotel Victoria (304 E. 9th Street) are the St. Peter and Paul's Catholic Church, 9th and McGee Street and the Grand Avenue Methodist Church, 9th and Grand Avenue. The White House Hotel was located at 744 Oak Street. (Val B. Mintun Collection)

Kansas City, Missouri – Circa 1891
This is believed to be an abandoned cemetery in the West Bottoms of Kansas City, Missouri. A garden has been planted in front of the gate. There are five headstones that can be seen on the right hand side of the tree that is in the middle cemetery. I did not make an extensive search for the location of this cemetery. (Val B. Mintun Collection)

Kansas City, Missouri – Circa 1892
Mr. Mintun did not provide a location or any information about this house. Close examination indicates the house is vacant and preparations are being made to move or demolish this house. (Val.B. Mintun Collection)

Kansas City, Missouri – Circa 1891
Looking south at 8th Street and Grand Avenue. The building in the fore-ground is on the southeast corner of 8th Street and Grand Avenue. Is also the office and residence of Dr. Flavel B. Tiffany. (Two streets in Kansas City North, Tiffany Springs Road and Tiffany Parkway were named for him. The former town of Tiffany Springs, Missouri was also named for him.) The tall building in the top left-hand corner of the photograph is the Hotel Victoria, 304 E. 9th street. This photograph shows how the square block area looked before condemnation and excavation began in 1893 to build the U.S. Post Office and Customs House. (Val B. Mintun Collection)

Kansas City, Missouri – Circa 1891

This photo was taken from the roof of the Rialto building on the Southwest corner of 9th and Grand Avenue. (This square block area will be vacated for the 2nd U.S. Post Office and Customs House (completed in 1896, and demolished in 1938). The office building and residence of Dr. Flavel B. Tiffany is on the southeast corner of 8th and Grand. The Hotel Victoria, located at 304 E. 9th Street, is in the upper right hand corner of the photo. Notice the wooden sidewalk on the east side of Grand Avenue. The next page will show what happened to all the buildings. (Val B. Mintun Collection)

U.S. Court House & Post Office 1900 to 1933

Kansas City, Missouri – May 1, 1893

(View 1 of 3 Views) This photo was taken from the roof of the Rialto building located on the southwest corner of 9th and Grand Avenue looking northeast. The wooden fence surrounds a square block area with Grand Avenue on the west, 9th Street on the South, McGee Street on the east and 8th Street on the north. The ground has been cleared and excavation of the foundation has been started for the U.S. Post Office and Customs House. The Hotel Victoria(top right hand corner) 304 E. 9th Street was built in 1888 and destroyed by fire February 12, 1960. (Val B. Mintun Collection)

Kansas City, Missouri – 1893
(View 2 of 3 Views) Looking south from the north gate located on the southwest corner of 8th and Grand Avenue. Most of the Rialto building located at 9th and Grand is shown on the right side of photo. The Grand Avenue Methodist Church is across from the Rialto building at 901 Grand Avenue. Saint Peter and Paul's Catholic Church, 900 McGee Street, is shown behind the Grand Avenue Methodist Church. (Val B. Mintun Collection)

Kansas City, Missouri - 1893

(View 3 of 3 Views) Looking southwest from the middle of 8th Street between McGee Street and Grand Avenue. The men in the fore-ground are excavating for the foundation of the new U.S. Post Office and Customs House. The following buildings are shown in this photo: (1.) The Keith and Perry office building, 902 Walnut Street built in 1887; (2.) The U.S. Courthouse, 901 Walnut Street built in 1884; (3.) The Rialto Building, 901 Grand Avenue destroyed by fire in 1908; (4.) The Grand Avenue Methodist Church, 901 Grand Avenue built in 1870; and (5.) The St. Peter and Paul's Catholic Church, southeast corner of 9th and McGee Street built in 1884. (Val B. Mintun Collection)

Kansas City, Missouri - 1893
Looking northwest from 10th Street and Grand Avenue. The following buildings have been identified in this photo, they are: (1.) New York Life Building 8th and Baltimore Street; (2.) Keith and Perry Building southwest corner 9th Walnut Street; and (3.) U.S. Court House southeast corner 9th and Walnut Street. (Val B. Mintun Collection)

Kansas City, Missouri - 1893
The steamboat A. L. Mason, a river freighter shown docking in Kansas City, Missouri. The A. L. Mason operated between Kansas City and New Orleans. (Val B. Mintun Collection)

Kansas City Missouri – Circa 1893
The intersection of 10th and Main Streets, looking north from the west side of Main Street. (Val B. Mintun Photograph)

Kansas City, Missouri – Circa 1890
The intersection of 10th and Main Streets, looking south from the west side of Main Street. (Val B. Mintun Photograph)

Kansas City, Missouri – August 8, 1894, Wednesday a.m.
Mr. Mintun was born August 28, 1874 and he may have been born in this house. His obituary states he was born near the President Hotel, 14th and Baltimore Street. The address of this residence was 1313 Baltimore Street. He did not identify the family in this photo. (Val B. Mintun Photograph)

Kansas City, Missouri – Circa 1906
This is a photograph of the Elm Ridge Race Track and Club House that opened for horse racing in April of 1904. The track was located one block east of The Paseo Blvd. from 59th to 63rd streets. Horse racing in the State of Missouri was outlawed by the State Legislature in 1906 and the track closed down. In 1912 the race track and club house were purchased by the newly formed Blue Hills Club. (Val B. Mintun Photograph)

Kansas City, Missouri – 1912
Former President Theodore Roosevelt campaigning in Kansas City in 1912. The parade is going north on Grand Avenue. The businesses in the background are the Corn Belt Bank, 1019 Grand Avenue and the F.G. Smith Piano Co., 1013-1015 Grand Avenue. (Val B. Mintun Photograph)

Kansas City, Missouri – 1913 – View 1 of 5 Views
Members of the Kansas City Missouri Fire Department marching in a parade during Fire Prevention Week of October 1913. They are marching north on Grand Avenue in downtown Kansas City. (Val B. Mintun Photograph)

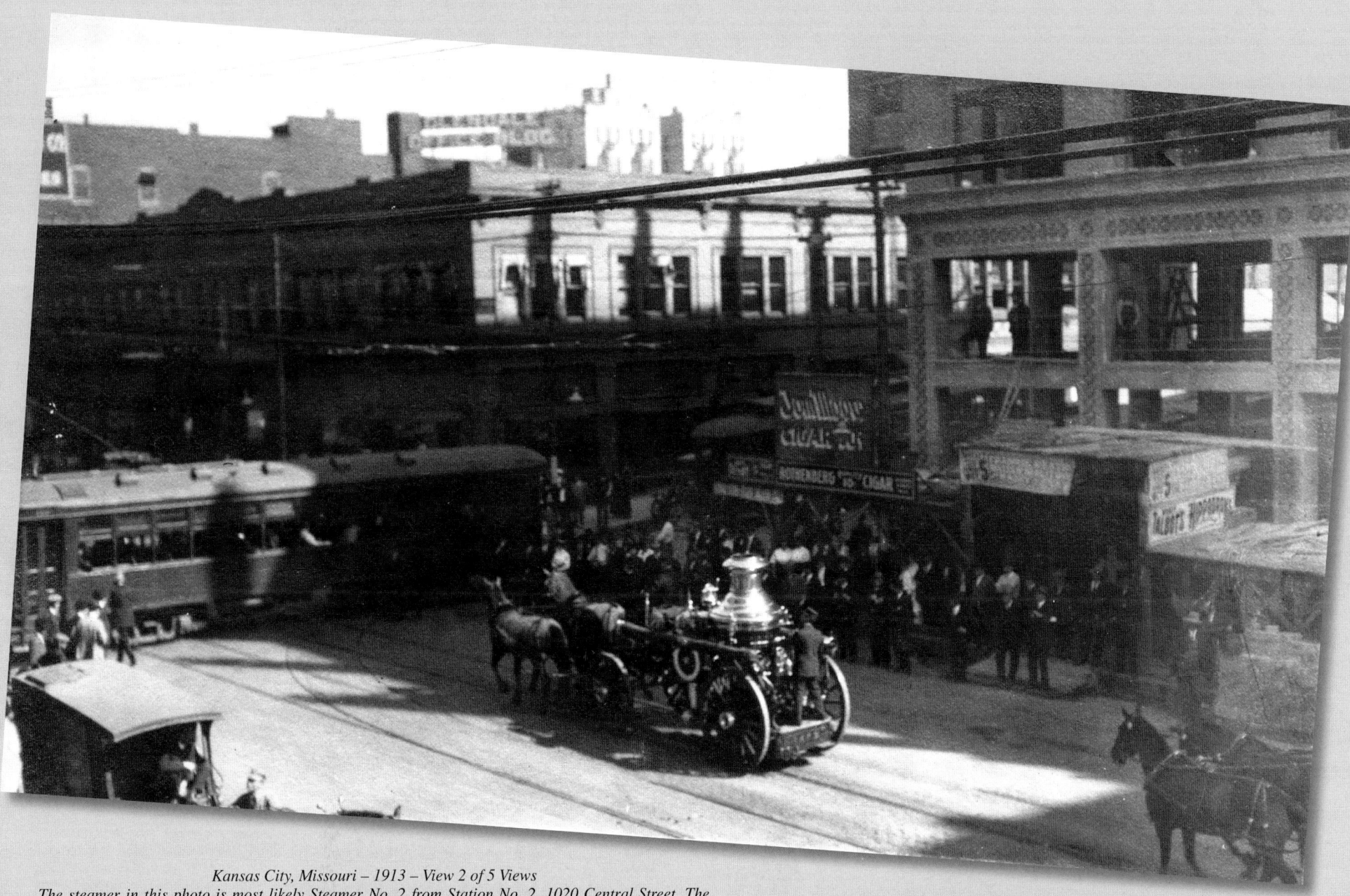

Kansas City, Missouri – 1913 – View 2 of 5 Views
The steamer in this photo is most likely Steamer No. 2 from Station No. 2, 1020 Central Street. The steamer is waiting for the trolley car, going east, to clear the intersection. (Val B. Mintun Photograph)

Kansas City, Missouri – 1913 – View 3 of 5 Views
Aerial Truck No. 1 from Station No. 2, 1020 Central Street is following Steamer No. 2 in the Fire Prevention parade. (Val B. Mintun Photograph)

Kansas City, Missouri – 1913 – View 4 of 5 Views
The Kansas City, Missouri Fire Department invited the Kansas City, Kansas Fire Department to be part of their Fire Prevention parade.
Kansas City, Kansas sent their new 1913 Kissel ladder service truck. The truck is north bound on Grand Avenue. (Val B. Mintun Photograph)

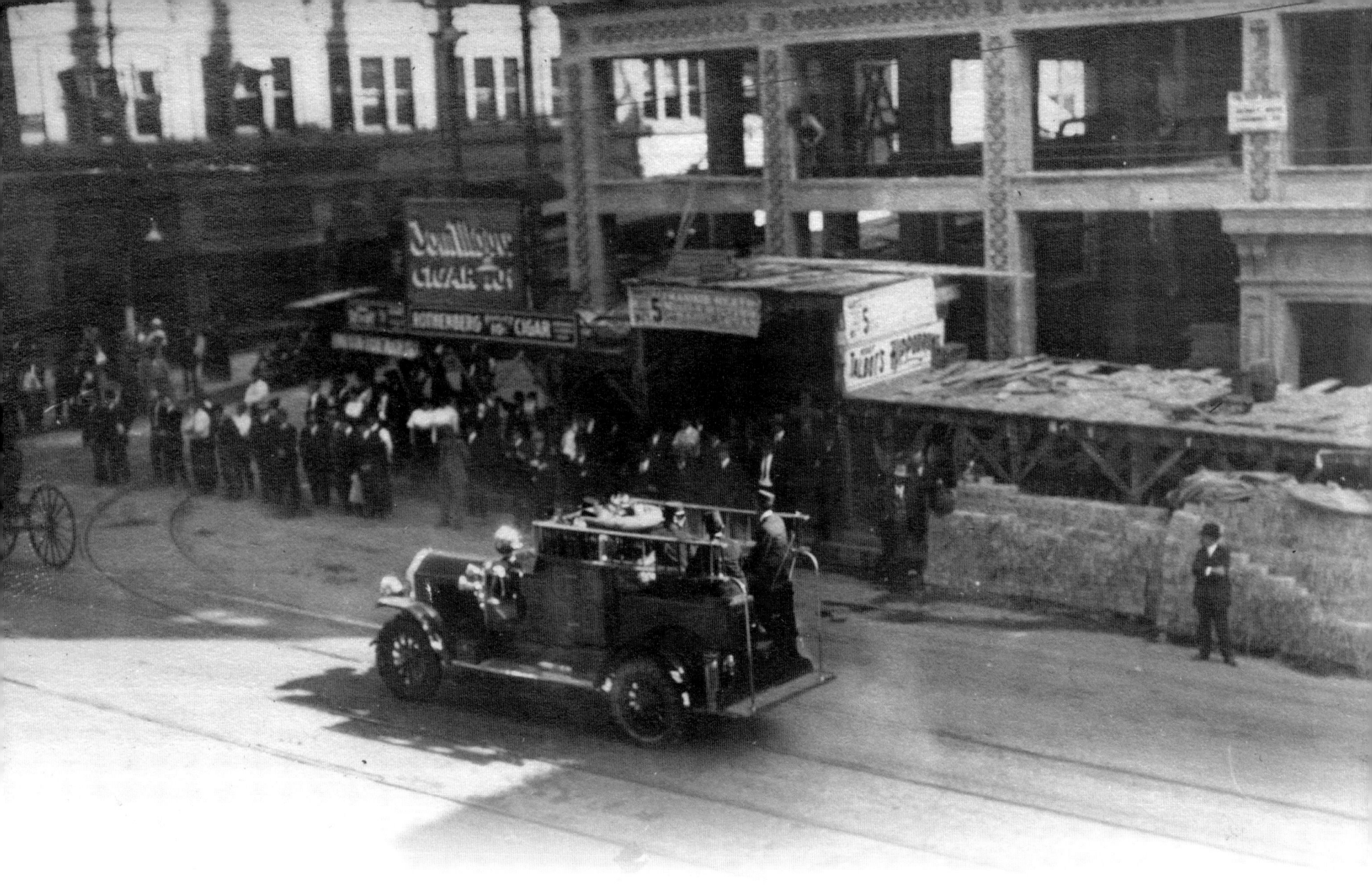

Kansas City, Missouri – 1913 – View 5 of 5 Views
The Kansas City, Kansas Fire Department also sent a hose and chemical truck to be in the parade. (Val B. Mintun Photograph)

This photo shows Northeast High School, 415 Van Brunt Boulevard under construction in 1913. The school opened May 4, 1914. (Val B. Mintun Photograph)

The Spanish Cannon at 12th and The Paseo was a gift from the U.S. Government to the Kansas City Park Board August 22, 1899. This photo was taken of Mr. Mintun and family in 1913. (Val B. Mintun Photograph)

Kansas City, Missouri – 1913
Pershing Road and Main Street was the location of the new Union Station. The building was completed and the opening and dedication was October 29, 1914. (Val B. Mintun Photograph)

Kansas City, Missouri – 1913
Looking north at the east side of Grand Avenue and 10th Street. The tall white building is the newly constructed Grand Avenue Temple Office building at 901 Grand Avenue. The Bailey-Reynolds Co. address was 913-15 Grand Avenue. The building behind Temple Office building is the U.S. Post Office and Customs House. (Val. B. Mintun Photograph)

Kansas City, Missouri – Circa 1913
The 9-story building, shown on the left, is the Robert Keith Furniture and Carpet Co. and was located on the southeast corner of 11th and Grand Avenue. This photo was taken from the roof of a 5 Story Building at 1016 Grand Avenue. The automobile going west on 11th Street could be the same one pictured in the photograph below. (Val B. Mintun Photograph)

Two members of the Mintun family with their 1912 battery operated Baker automobile. (Val B. Mintun Photograph)

July 20, 1914 – Unable to locate the Holker's Grove Telephone Co. or where the picnic was held. Mr. Holly Jarboe (in photo) has two Kansas City Streets named after him, Holly and Jarboe streets. This was done by a family member who purchased and platted the Jarboe Addition in November of 1870. The boundary of the addition was 17th Street on the north, Summit Street on the east, 20th Street on the south and Holly Street on the west. (Val B. Mintun Photograph)

Kansas City, Missouri – Circa 1914
Looking north on Walnut Street from 8th Street. The dress of the people indicates it is summertime. The Luce Trunk Factory is the first building on the left and the Rainshine Umbrella Co. is on the right side of the photo. (Val B. Mintun Photograph)

Kansas City, Missouri – Circa 1913
Aaron Montgomery Ward of Chicago, Illinois opened a new catalog mail-order building in 1914. The building was located on the northeast corner of St. John Avenue and Belmont Blvd. Upon completion it was said to be a half-a-mile around the outside walls, with 47,000 panes of glass. It was also known as the largest building west of the Mississippi River. (Val B. Mintun Photograph)

Kansas City, Missouri – Circa 1914 – 12th Street Viaduct
This is a new major thoroughfare under construction leading to the City's Central Industrial District. It was first called the "French Bottoms" then the "West Bottoms". The term Central Industrial District never caught on and it is still referred as the West Bottoms. This viaduct opened March 18, 1915. (Val B. Mintun Photograph)

Kansas City, Missouri – 1915
The Coates Opera House was destroyed by fire in 1900 leaving the city without an opera house. Mr. Willis Wood of St. Joseph, Missouri came to Kansas City in 1901 and began construction on a new opera house known as the Willis Wood Theatre at 11th and Baltimore. The theatre was completed in 1902 with a tunnel connecting to the Baltimore Hotel at 12th and Baltimore. The Coates House Hotel and the Coates Opera House also had a connecting tunnel. The hotel and opera house were on the southeast and northwest corners of 10th and Broadway. (Val B. Mintun Photograph)

Kansas City, Missouri – March 17, 1920
This is a view of the southwest corner of 14th and Main Streets. The buildings in this photo will all be demolished and construction will begin on the Main Street Theater. The theater opened for business October 30, 1921. (Val B. Mintun Photograph)

Kansas City, Missouri – March 17, 1920
Looking northeast from the west side of Baltimore Avenue near 14th Street. The address of the building being torn down is 1321 Baltimore Avenue. The south side and west end of the Duff and Repp Furniture and Carpet building can be seen in this photo. The address of this business was 1216 Main Street. (Photo by Val B. Mintun)

Kansas City, Missouri – March 17, 1920
This photo was taken looking north on Baltimore Avenue. Mr. Mintun was standing on the east side of Baltimore and just south of 14th Street. The building under construction is the Kansas City Club. Construction began in 1917 but stopped during World War I and completed in 1920. This building replaced the former location of the Kansas City Club on the northeast corner of 12th and Wyandotte. The horse drawn delivery wagon and the truck hauling demolition materials shown on the previous page can also be seen in this photo graph. (Val B. Mintun Photograph)

Kansas City, Missouri – April 1917
This is the former residence of "Wash" Adams, 324 E. 11th Street. The house will be torn down and the new Telephone Building will be built on the same site. (Photo by Val. B. Mintun)

Kansas City, Missouri – Circa 1920 – The Telephone Building, 324 E. 11th Street. This photograph was taken by the Tyner and Murphy Photograph Co. Their photographer took this photo from the roof of the building on the southeast corner of 11th and Oak Streets. The photo was taken sometime after the completion of the building in 1920. There is a person looking out the window on the 4th floor, east side of the building observing traffic on Oak Street Mr. Mintun was given or purchased this photo from the Tyner & Murphy Co. (Photo by Val. B. Mintun)

Kansas City, Missouri – 1926
The two women and the child in the photograph are walking north on Oak Street and about to cross 11th Street. Mr. Mintun took this photo from one of the lower floors of the Telephone building 324 East 11th Street. The second billboard from the left, advertising the movie "The Show Off" was released in 1926. The small white building advertising "Hamburgers 5 cents" is White Castle Hamburger Stand. All the buildings on the east side of Oak Street will be torn down and the present City Hall of Kansas City, Missouri will open October 25, 1937. (Val B. Mintun Photograph)

Kansas City, Missouri – June 17, 1926
This photo was taken from one of the upper floors on the south side of the Telephone Building at 324 E. 11th Street. The Street is Oak street and it ends at the railroad tracks near 22nd street. (Val B. Mintun Photograph)

Kansas City, Missouri – 1928
Adding 14 additional floors to the Telephone Building 324 E. 11th Street in 1928. Mr. Mintun was standing on the east side of 11th Street between Locust and Cherry to take this photograph. (Val B. Mintun Photograph)

Kansas City, Missouri – 1929
This photograph shows the completion of adding 14 floors to the Telephone Building in 1929. Mr. Mintun purchased or was given this photograph from the Anderson Photograph Co., 912 Grand Avenue. (Val B. Mintun Collection)

Kansas City, Missouri – 1931
This is a panoramic view looking southwest from one of the upper floors of the Telephone Building 324 E. 11th Street. The two predominant buildings in this photograph are: The Bryant Building (right side of photo) and the Kansas City Power & Light Building (on the left side of the photo). The Bryant building was completed in 1931 and was 331 feet tall. The Kansas City Power and Light Building was completed in 1931 and was the tallest building in the State of Missouri at 379.5 ft. There is still construction scaffolding attached to the east side of the building. (Val B. Mintun Photograph)

Kansas City, Missouri – No. 1 of 2 Post Cards
This post card is one of the two post cards from Mr. Mintun's collection of photographs. On July 3, 1869 the citizens of Kansas City turned out in great numbers to see the first train cross the Missouri River into Kansas City. Construction of this bridge began in 1867. The original name of this bridge was the "Kansas City Bridge" but gave way to the "Hannibal Bridge" as the Hannibal and St. Joseph Railroad was first to use the bridge. The bridge also served as a toll bridge for people traveling by foot, horseback or in horse drawn wagons. The toll started at 5 cents (people walking) and went up. The original bridge was torn down in 1915 and a new bridge was built 100 feet down stream and opened in 1917. You can view this bridge when traveling north bound on the Broadway Bridge. (Val B. Mintun Collection)

Building Hannibal Bridge – Mo. Side – Aug 1867.

Kansas City, Missouri – No. 2 of 2 Post Cards
November 1, 1921 the Allied Commanders of World War I were invited to Kansas City to lay the corner stone and the dedication of the land to build the Liberty Memorial. The photographer hand painted the names of each officer and date on the photo. The only legible name is Admiral Beatty. Mr. Mintun put their names on the other side of this post card. The names of the officers from left to right are: General Jacques, (Belgium) General Diaz, (Italy) Marshall Foch, (France) General Pershing, (U.S.A.) and Admiral Beatty. (England) This post card was made available for purchase in 1922. (Val B. Mintun Collection)